art in action¹

First edition for the United States, its territories and dependencies, and Canada published in 2010 by Barron's Educational Series, Inc.

Copyright © 2010 Elwin Street Productions
Conceived and produced by Elwin Street Productions
144 Liverpool Road
London N1 1 LA
United Kingdom
www.elwinstreet.com

All inquiries should be addressed to:
Barron's Educational Series, Inc.
250 Wireless Blvd.
Hauppauge, NY 11788
www.barronseduc.com

ISBN-13: 978-0-7641-4440-0
ISBN-10: 0-7641-4440-5

Library of Congress Control Number: 2009940230

Printer Reference Number: 998809/0110/Singapore

The activities described in this book are to be carried out with parental supervision at all times. Every effort has been made to ensure the safety of the activities detailed. Neither the author nor the publishers shall be liable or responsible for any harm or damage done allegedly arising from any information or suggestion in this book.

Picture credits
Henri Matisse, *The Snail*, The Art Archive/Tate Gallery London/Eileen Tweedy, cover, 13; Seth Joel/Getty Image, cover; Chris Rout/Alamy, 7; Juice Images/Corbis 8; Georges Seurat, *The Circus*, The Art Archive/Musée d'Orsay Paris/Alfredo Dagli Orti, 10, 19; Lipunja, *Aboriginal Bark Painting*, The Art Archive/Musée des Arts Africans et Océaniens/Alfredo Dagli Orti, 25; Albrecht Dürer, *Portrait of Bernhard von Reesen*, The Art Archive/Gemaldegalerie Dresden, 30, 39; Whistler, *Symphony in White No III*, © The Barber Institute of Fine Arts, University of Birmingham/The Bridgeman Art Library UK, 33; Jakob van der Schley, *Buffel, Buffle*, The Art Archive/Gift of the Coe Foundation/Buffalo Bill Historical Center, Cody, Wyoming, USA, 45; Theo van Doesburg, *Composition*, The Art Archive/Peggy Guggenheim Collection Venice/Gianni Dagli Orti, 50, 59; Juan Gris, *Nature Morte; violon et verre*, The Art Archive/Musée National d'Art Moderne Paris/Gianni Dagli Orti, 53; Kazimir Malevich, *Suprematist Composition*, The Art Archive/Peggy Guggenheim Collection Venice/Gianni Dagli Orti, 65; George Stubbs, *A Couple of Fox Hounds*, The Art Archive/Tate Gallery London/Eileen Tweedy, 70, 85; Henri Rousseau, *Surprised!*, The Art Archive/National Gallery London/Eileen Tweedy, 73; Jacopo Zucchi, *Pergola with Birds*, The Art Archive/ Villa Medici Rome/Gianni Dagli Orti, 79.

Art Director and Designer: Simon Daley
Original Photography: Ian Garlick

Printed in Singapore
9 8 7 6 5 4 3 2 1

art in action[1]

Introducing children to
the world of Western
art with 24 creative
projects inspired by
12 masterpieces

Maja Pitamic

BARRON'S

Contents

Discover art with children
by Mike Norris

It's no news that parents and children are hard pressed to find the time to get to know each other better. If parents aren't spending the best part of the week commuting to work, accomplishing that work, then returning home—and this is often true for both parents—they are taking their children to a dizzying array of after-school activities. There, they give what support they can, but it mainly consists of either watching the child or being a one-way street of encouragement. And, alluring new technologies have grown stronger and more numerous reducing family time further. They used to be limited to the telephone, radio, and television. But now even television, a worry to sociologists for decades, can be considered a social experience compared to the essentially isolating pursuits of the Internet, video games, and text messaging. So what can a family do to play together, have fun together, and, in the process, learn about each other?

Art in Action is an answer. Art can bring parent and child together to learn and discuss, and the paintings in this book have a significant power to bring people together. This volume takes aim at the overwhelming desire of children to experiment with and manipulate materials to express themselves, although, as the picture on the book's cover indicates, children can also be struck by the aesthetic power of an original work of art. The activities in *Art in Action* bring parents and children into a learning environment stocked with fun; they are calibrated to the expression of creativity, not pegged to the differing abilities of family members. One cannot, of course, ask a five-year-old child to be master of the materials and techniques of a famous oil painter. But the genius of this book is that each activity—designed for the skills of children aged between five and eight—extends logically from the original artwork, no matter what its medium, providing refreshing insights about painters and painting.

Mike Norris has been a staff educator at The Metropolitan Museum of Art for over fifteen years and oversees the teaching in the Met's programs for families at the Main Building in Manhattan.

Introduction

Time after time I am bowled over by children's responses to paintings. They see with a directness and freshness that seems far removed from the world of art. On one occasion I was looking at Van Gogh's *Starry Night* with my class. I asked them why they thought Van Gogh had chosen to paint the sky in that particular way. After several very observant answers, a four-year-old girl put her hand up and said, "Because he wanted to show us how beautiful the world is." Countless books have been written about Van Gogh and yet a four-year-old can sum up in one sentence the purpose and intent of his paintings.

I hope that your children will similarly delight and amaze you with some of their responses to the paintings they see. Along the way you will also come to understand how they perceive the world around them by their responses. The art activities inspired directly from the paintings will allow your children to explore and develop their own creative skills and talents.

This book will enable you to introduce the world of art to your child but relax, no prior knowledge of the subject is needed. Each painting comes with a brief introduction, followed by suggestions for questions the painting may inspire and art activities. The art activities use materials that are readily available and they come with clear step-by-step instructions. You don't need to start at Chapter 1 and work your way through. Let your child choose which picture or activity appeals to them the most and work from there.

A note on art supplies and preparation

- All of the art supplies listed in the activities in this book should be easily obtainable from supermarkets, art stores, and hardware stores.
- It is advisable to cover the area you are working in with a waterproof sheet before you start any art activity.
- It is probably a good idea to cover up in an old T-shirt or shirt before activities get messy.

1 Color

Imagine a day without color. How different would your life be? Color fills every part of our lives and so we tend to take it for granted. Each color produces its own set of moods and feelings. Yet colors don't just work in isolation—when put alongside other colors they can create a whole new drama and dynamism of emotions. It is this that artists tap into when they use color in their paintings. So in this chapter we have the bold, intense blocks of color in Matisse's *The Snail*, the primary colors, applied in dots, of Seurat's action painting *The Circus*, and the subtle earth tones of Lipunja's *Aboriginal Bark Painting*.

Snail squares

If you had to choose only one painting in the world to represent color then it would have to be Matisse's *The Snail*. Matisse has distilled the very essence of color into this picture. You may think that in creating an abstract (not realistic) work composed of a pattern of blocks of color there would be little to attract our attention. But you would be surprised how this picture reaches out to people, drawing them in and capturing their imagination.

What's the story?

To find the story behind this painting you have to look at Matisse's life. The first thing to consider is the painting's size; it measures just over 9 x 9ft (2.7 x 2.7m). You can pace this out on the floor. It's huge! The picture was produced on this scale not only for aesthetic reasons but for practical ones too. Matisse worked well into his eighties and had to battle with failing eyesight. *The Snail* was created a year before Matisse died and is on a monumental scale so that he could see the picture he was working on.

The blocks of color are torn pieces of paper painted with gouache paint. The blocks were arranged onto a white canvas by Matisse and his assistants. Look at the picture with half-closed eyes. You will discover that even with this limited view, the colors zing out of the canvas.

Matisse wanted to create art despite his physical limitations and this fact seems to intrigue people the most about this painting. If you want to understand Matisse's failing eyesight and his continuing desire to paint just think about any time you have wanted to do something new and the determination it has taken to achieve your goal.

The Snail	
Artist	Henri Matisse
Nationality	French
Painted	1953

Think about. . .

Why did Matisse use bright colors instead of snail-like colors?
Would this picture have had the same impact if it had been made with brown tones? Matisse was continually experimenting with color and how different colors make us feel.

Can you see the snail hiding in the picture?
Look very closely at the colored blocks. Do you see the small snail in the mauve block?

Why did Matisse choose a snail?
Perhaps for the beautiful shape of its spiral shell—it's such a dynamic shape, where does it start and where does it end?

Project **Tissue-paper picture**

The main material used in this art activity is tissue paper. Tissue paper has the advantage of being very easy to tear and it also has a pleasing, tactile feel—when torn it has a wonderful raggedy edge.

1 Lay your ruler down on a piece of tissue. Tear the tissue into strips down the length of the ruler. These strips will be the border of your picture.

2 Now tear the tissue into about ten rough 4-in (10-cm) squares. Make sure you have an even mix of colors.

3 Arrange the tissue-paper squares on the white heavy paper. Experiment with the position of the pieces of tissue until you are satisfied with the composition.

4 Use the glue stick to stick the tissue paper down. Don't stick the tissue paper completely down, leave some of the edges free—this gives an extra three-dimensional feel to your picture.

You will need

A ruler

A selection of brightly-colored tissue paper

One sheet of 11 x 17in (A2) heavy white paper or larger if you want

A glue stick

Project **Color tones**

By gradually adding more and more of a color
to white paint you can slowly darken it through
a series of tones.

1 Working horizontally, mark off the canvas at 1½-in (4-cm) intervals using your pencil and ruler. Place the tape in a horizontal line below the first 1½-in (4-cm) marking.

2 Put some white paint onto the plate and mix in the tiniest amount of your favorite color. Now apply the paint to the empty band of canvas above the masking tape.

3 Move the masking tape down to the next 1½-in (4-cm) mark.

4 Add some more of your chosen color to the white paint to make a darker shade and then apply the paint to the next empty band of canvas. Continue until you reach the bottom of the canvas.

You will need

A mounted canvas, any size will do

A pencil

A ruler

A piece of masking tape slightly longer than the length of the canvas

White paint

Your favorite color of poster or acrylic paint

A plate for mixing the tones

A square-ended paintbrush, about 1in (2.5cm) thick, plus another paintbrush for mixing the tones

Top tip

You might need a rough piece of paper to try out the colors before you put them on the canvas.

Dot painting

Seurat's painting of the circus captures that split second in time, that gasp of amazement from the crowd, as the dancer impossibly balances on the back of the prancing pony and the acrobat is caught mid-tumble. The dynamic energy of the performers is contrasted with the stillness of the crowd. The overall impression of the painting is fantastical—like something remembered from a dream.

What's the story?

Born in Paris in 1859, Seurat trained at the École des Beaux-Arts and as a student he studied the scientific work of the chemist Michel Eugène Chevreul. Chevreul looked at optics and color and particularly at the division of light into primary colors (red, yellow, and blue). This was to form the basis of Seurat's painting style, known as Pointillism or, as he preferred to call it, Divisionism. Seurat put tiny dots of unmixed color next to each other on a white background so that from a distance they fuse together in the viewer's eye to give the appearance of other colors. As well as using a scientific basis for his exploration of color in painting, Seurat also tried to find scientific ways of painting the most harmonious lines.

The Circus was Seurat's final work. Considered unfinished, The Circus combined his interest in both color and line. We are in a ringside seat, getting only a glimpse of the blurred faces of the performers as they speed past, similar to the image a camera takes as it captures moving objects. The echoing shapes of the performers' bodies, the use of the orange tones, which link the audience and performers together, and the yellow scarf the clown holds, leads your eye out of the picture and then pulls you back in again. Seurat's use of color and line are a balancing act which are as poised as the dancer on the back of the pony.

The Circus	
Artist	Georges Seurat
Nationality	French
Painted	1891

Think about. . .

Why did Seurat apply the paint in dots of pure color?
He wanted to reproduce colors as they appear in nature, something artists of earlier generations had been attempting to do. It's our eyes that blend individual colors together.

The performers link up to make a diamond shape. What effect does this have on the painting?
The diamond shape unifies the painting. The shapes are echoed and repeated—the figure of the acrobat is repeated in the figure of the ringmaster which is further emphasized by the scarf that wraps around him.

Project **Spray picture**

This art project recreates Pointillism using stencils and paint. The paint is applied by using a toothbrush and flicking the bristles. The paint is laid on in individual colors which build up to produce a final unified effect.

1 Begin by creating your stencils. Sketch the circus figures onto your card. You can trace the characters from Seurat's painting on page 19 or create some of your own. Cut out and set aside.

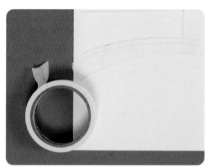

2 On your plain paper sketch out the circus ring, doorway, and rows of seating. Use the masking tape and cut out strips to cover these areas.

You will need

A sheet of white posterboard for the stencils

A pencil

A pair of scissors

A sheet of white heavy paper, any size

Masking tape

An old toothbrush

Ready mixed or powder paint in orange, yellow, red, and blue

A paintbrush for mixing

A ruler, or you could use your finger

3 Arrange the stencils on the plain paper and get all of your paints ready. Spend some time mixing the paints to get colors you are happy with. Dip your toothbrush in the yellow paint and hold it over the paper. Pull your ruler or finger across the bristles towards you—this will make the paint spray away from you. Move the toothbrush around the paper so that the paint is evenly applied.

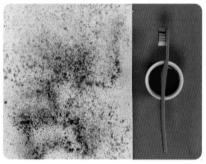

4 Clean your toothbrush and repeat step 3 with another color. Keep working this way until you have used all your colors. Use strong colors, like orange, with care as they can overpower the painting. When you are using a darker color look at how Seurat used dark colors to create shadows around the figures. When the paint is dry carefully remove the masking tape and the stencils.

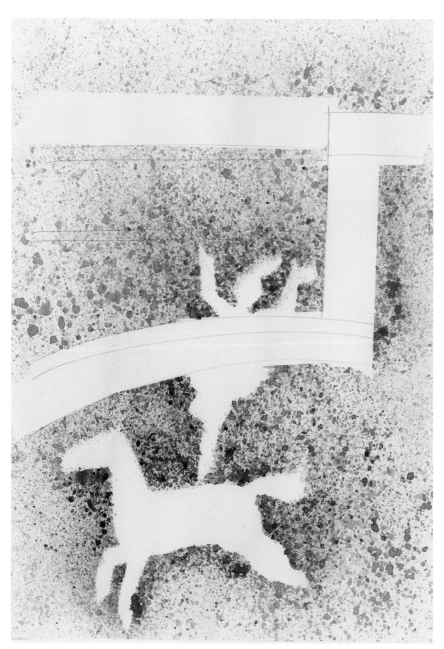

Top tips

- Try the toothbrush spray action on a piece of paper before using it on your painting.
- Make sure you keep the stencils still while you apply the paint.
- Don't overload the toothbrush or it will drip.
- Work slowly and keep checking that there is an even balance between all the colors.

Project **Dot picture**

This is the cheat's version of Pointillism because it imitates the style of Pointillism without involving any of the hard work. Fine sandpaper and wax crayons are used to make the original picture then it is transferred onto plain paper using a lukewarm iron. The texture of the sandpaper is picked up by the transfer and gives the impression of Pointillism.

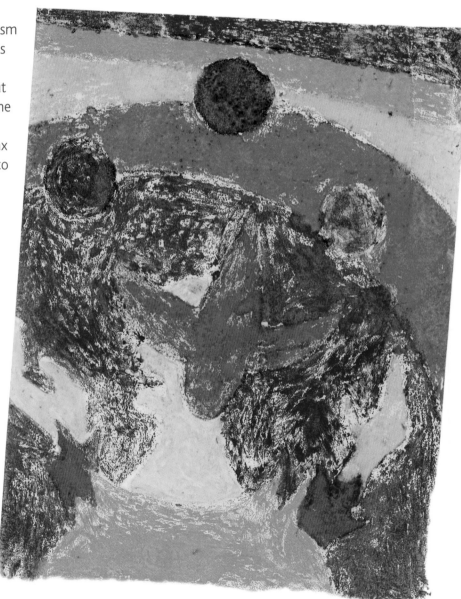

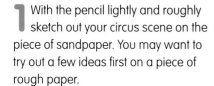

1 With the pencil lightly and roughly sketch out your circus scene on the piece of sandpaper. You may want to try out a few ideas first on a piece of rough paper.

2 When you are happy with your drawing begin to color it in using your wax crayons. Press quite hard when you are coloring and make sure that no bits of sandpaper show through as this will affect the quality of the finished picture.

You will need

A sheet of fine sandpaper, roughly 8½ x 11in (A4) size

A pencil

Assorted wax crayons

A sheet of 8½ x 11in (A4) white heavy paper

A lukewarm iron

3 Place your finished sandpaper picture face up onto an ironing board. Put a plain piece of paper over the top. With an adult, iron over the top of the plain paper with a luke-warm iron.

4 Lift up the plain piece of paper and you will find that your sandpaper picture has been magically transferred onto the plain paper.

Earth pigments

In Lipunja's abstract painting representing the body there aren't any dazzling blocks of color, such as you would see in a work by an artist like Henri Matisse. The colors Lipunja used came from his world and landscape—earth tones, reds, whites, and ochre. Lipunja demonstrated that subdued colors, when subtly used, can be just as compelling as bright primary colors. You could have found this painting in the chapter in this book on Shape as well as here, in Color, because there is complete harmony between the colors used and the composition.

What's the story?

We know very little about Lipunja because for him, and other Aboriginal artists, his art was not about individual fame but about a celebration of the whole of Aboriginal life. Lipunja painted all that was dear and sacred to him—earth, water, animals, and the worship of ancestor spirits.

Aboriginal art came to be known in America and Europe during the earlier part of the twentieth century and there is evidence that Pablo Picasso was influenced by it. Lipunja and his fellow artists from Arnhem Land came to prominence during the 1960s and their work is now exhibited in galleries around the world.

Lipunja's studio was probably outside and the materials he used were taken from the natural world. Instead of a canvas he used a piece of bark so the picture has a wonderful texture which makes the paint seem to shimmer. There is perfect balance between the shapes, which creates a sense of movement. Perhaps the most appealing aspect of this painting is the sense of timelessness that it conveys. The colors and shapes used are as old as the Aboriginal peoples themselves—perhaps this is why Lipunja's painting is truly great.

Aboriginal Bark Painting

Artist	Lipunja
Nationality	Aboriginal Australian
Painted	c.1960s

Think about...

Why did Lipunja draw the human body in this way?
Aboriginal artists use symbols to represent figures, animals, and the landscape, e.g. a wavy line stands for running water.

How was the bark prepared?
A section of bark would have been taken from the tree and the outer bark removed. The inner "skin" was then smoothed and sanded down. The bark was then weighed down to flatten it.

How was the paint put on?
With feathers, chewed-up bits of bark, and twigs.

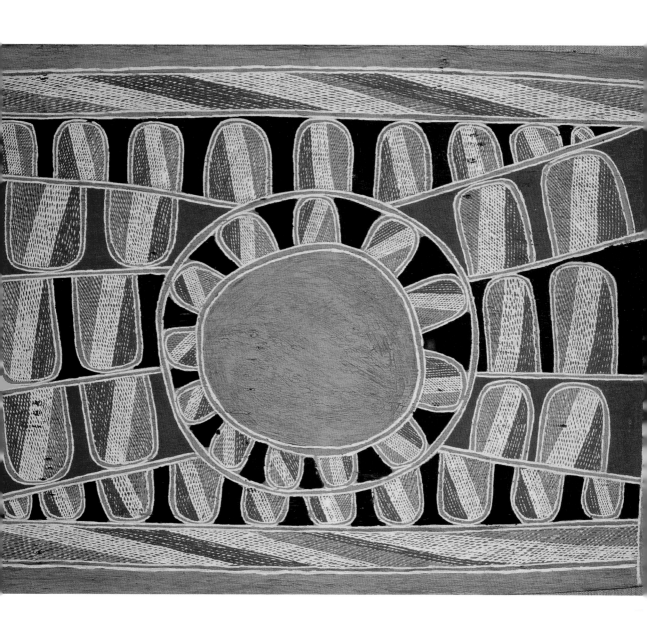

"This picture makes me happy because it's got so much sun in it."

Tilly, age 5

Project **Tie-dye sunburst**

Aboriginals don't just use painting as a way of expressing their art but also as a way of decorating everyday objects. So in this art project we are going to use tie-dye to create a sunburst design on a fabric square that can be used as decoration—you could do several of these fabric squares in different colors and then join them together to make a patchwork wall hanging or cushion covers. Tie-dye is probably one of the oldest methods of fabric printing.

1 Cut your fabric into a square then fold it into quarters. Squeeze it down so that it looks like a closed umbrella. Tightly secure a rubber band around the open end of the fabric.

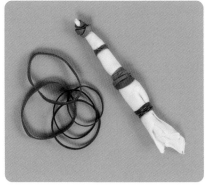

2 Evenly space the rest of the rubber bands down the fabric in the same way. The dye won't penetrate the fabric where the rubber bands are tight.

You will need

A piece of plain white or light-colored cotton (muslin works very well), about 8 x 8in (20 x 20cm)

A pair of scissors

Three or four rubber bands

A bucket

Water

Food coloring

An iron

A pair of tongs

A pair of rubber gloves

3 Put enough water in the bucket to cover the fabric and mix in the food coloring—how much depends on how strong you want the color to be. Wear gloves as dyes tend to leave permanent stains. Put the fabric into the bucket of dye and make sure that it is covered with the liquid.

4 You may need to use your tongs to push the fabric down so that it absorbs the liquid. Soak the fabric for several hours or overnight then take out of the dye. Throw away the dyed water and wash the bucket to prevent staining. Allow the fabric to dry out. Iron the fabric on a low heat then stand back and admire your work.

Top tip

Aborigines use natural dyes. If you want to use natural dyes, you could try any of the following: Beets, tea in bags, spinach, onions, or berries.

Project **Textures with paint**

Try your hand at painting your own Aboriginal-style painting. Use a cardboard comb to create the textural feel of the bark. Then layer a pattern over the top with some white paint.

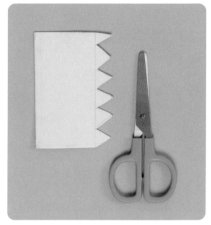

1 Draw a small zigzag line across your cardboard rectangle then cut along it. This is your paint comb.

2 Apply the paint to the white heavy paper using a paintbrush. Create a random pattern but lock the colors together, like the pieces of a jigsaw.

You will need

A small cardboard rectangle

A pencil

A pair of scissors

A sheet of white heavy paper, any size

A selection of poster or acrylic paints in earth shades, white, and brown

Medium- and thin-sized paintbrushs

A white or light-colored pencil

Rough sketch paper

A pencil

A cocktail stick or pencil

3 While the paint is still wet, take your paint comb and drag it across the paper. Don't worry if it's not perfectly straight, it will look more natural if it has a slight wave to it.

4 Draw a design with your pencil—the same one as Lipunja or something new. Then take a white or light-colored pencil and sketch your design onto your dry painted paper.

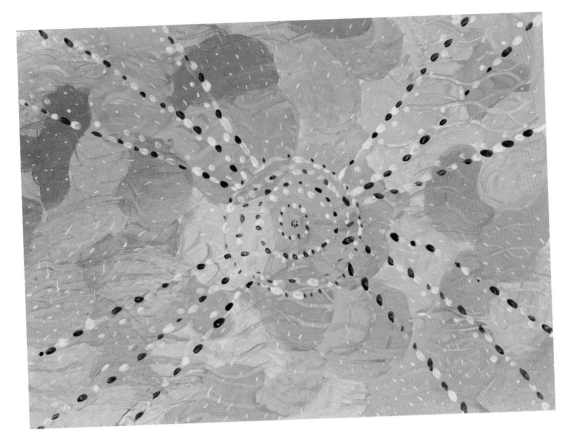

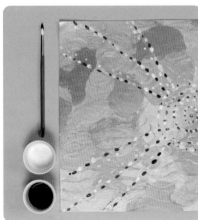

5 Take your white and dark brown paints and paint them over the top of your design.

6 Before the paint is dry use a cocktail stick to mark the paint in tiny left and right diagonals. This imitates the rough texture of Lipunja's bark painting.

Top tip

Apply the paint comb very lightly so that the grooves do not go too deep.

2 Black & white

Black and white—are they actually colors or tones or shades?
This argument has been going on for centuries and we still
haven't arrived at a definitive answer. But one thing is certain,
black, whether a color or a tone, follows a completely different
set of optical rules to all the other colors. White also has
special characteristics. One would think that working with just
black and white would restrict an artist but, as the selection of
pictures for this chapter demonstrates, it seems to stimulate
and challenge artists' imaginations.

Painting music

In Whistler's painting *Symphony in White No. III*, cool creams have been used to create a mood of lazy languor—you can almost feel the sultry heat as the two women recline in relaxed poses. Whistler used the color white to give the painting a tone and to make a harmonious whole.

Symphony in White No. III	
Artist James Abbott McNeill Whistler	
Nationality	American
Painted	1865–1867

What's the story?

Whistler was born in America in 1834 but moved to France in 1855 where he became a bohemian artist partying all night and sleeping until midday. This extreme behavior had unfortunate consequences on his health. Whilst in Paris he came into contact with artists of the Realist school, including Gustave Courbet. But it was his contact with the writer Theophile Gautier that was to prove most influential, for it was Gautier who believed in a link between art and music and this is what we see Whistler exploring in *Symphony in White No. III*. The painting was exhibited at the Royal Academy in London, where Whistler had moved in 1859. The women in the painting are a world away from the heavily corseted and upright figures seen in other Victorian paintings. They dreamily lean back with their loose hair and clothing reminiscent of medieval dress. But the women in Whistler's painting do not stand out as personalities—the folds of their dresses match the folds of the draped sofas—they are just a part of the tonal composition that makes up the "symphony" of the picture. The paint was applied with delicacy in tones of cream and white. A touch of the exotic was added with the foliage and the Japanese fan. The painting embodies Whistler's belief that beauty should be the overriding principle in the creation of art, he said, "Nature is very rarely right and must be improved upon by the artist with his own vision."

Think about. . .

Why don't the figures in Whistler's painting stand out as personalities?
Whistler didn't intend the women to stand out because for him they were just a part of the tonal composition he was trying to paint—he deliberately painted them in the same colors as the sofa they recline on.

How does the composition and design of the painting add to its mood?
There is very little space around the figures—it's almost as if they are hemmed in by the sofas. This reinforces the oppressive, humid atmosphere.

phony in White. Nº III. _Whistler. 1867_

"Looking at this picture makes me feel sleepy."

David, age 8

Project **Japanese fan**

Whistler collected Japanese prints and we can see their influence in his art. This next project is to make a fan, like the one in Whistler's painting.

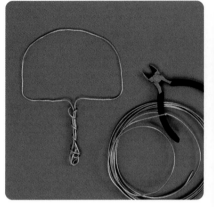

1 Cut the wire with pliers and then, using the pliers, bend the wire into a fan shape. Bring the two ends together and twist them around to form the handle part of the fan.

4 Using the glue stick, paste the butterflies onto each of the paper fan shapes.

2 Place your wire frame onto the paper and draw around it leaving a 1-in (2.5-cm) border. Repeat this step again so that you have two paper fan outlines. Cut out the paper fan shapes.

3 Fold both of the doilies in half and then draw half a butterfly on each one of them with your pencil. Cut out the butterfly shapes.

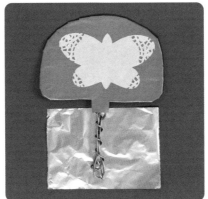

5 Turn the paper over and place the wire frame on top. Cut the paper at intervals all the way around the frame. Put the PVA glue onto the paper and glue around the frame. Repeat on the other side but trim the paper so that it doesn't overlap the first side.

6 Finish off by wrapping the handle with silver foil. If you want you can add silver paint or a color of your choice around the edge of the fan to frame the butterfly.

Top tip

Once the glue is on the fan, work quickly before it dries.

Project **Abstract picture**

In this art project you can recreate the effect of *Symphony in White No. III* as a purely abstract arrangement, so that the figures will be represented as curving shapes. To help you mix the tonal colors, pick up a couple of paint color strips (usually available free from hardware stores).

1 Look at Whistler's painting again—the women in the painting make S shapes with their bodies. Sketch out these S shapes in pencil on the paper then wet the paper all over with the paintbrush or small sponge.

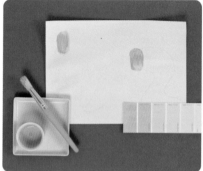

2 Take your yellow paint strips and find the darkest yellow in the painting that matches a color block on the strip. Now mix up that color and apply it vertically with one brushstroke width to each S shape, working from left to right.

You will need

A pencil

A sheet of watercolor or heavy paper, any size

A broad paintbrush or a small sponge

Two paint color strips (the kind you get in hardware stores)—one in gray-blue-white tones to match those found in Whistler's painting and one in yellow-cream-white tones

Watercolor paints or powder paints in white, blue, gray, yellow, lemon, and cream

3 Take the yellow color and lighten it one tone by adding white paint. Use the paint color strip to help you. Apply the paint in the same way putting the new color next to the first color so that both colors are together.

4 Continue to make the paint lighter and apply it in the same way until both shapes are filled.

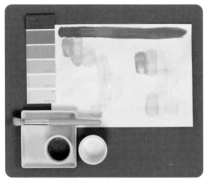

5 Clean your brush and mix up a gray/blue color to match that found in the bottom and top of Whistler's painting and, as before, match it to your color strip. Apply to the bottom and top of your paper in horizontal bands working in between the S shapes.

6 Lighten the color by adding some white paint, using the strip as your guide. Keep repeating this step working from the top to the bottom.

Top tips

• Don't completely soak the paper—it needs to be moist at all times but if it is too wet it will rip.

• Take time to mix the right color tone. If you are not sure about the color have a piece of paper on hand to test it out first.

Portrait power

In Dürer's *Portrait of Bernhard von Reesen*, black and white paint has been used in its purest form and everything in the picture has been pared down to create a portrait of elegant simplicity. There is nothing to distract your eye so the entire focus of your attention is drawn to the sitter's face. In this portrait's very simplicity, Dürer reveals his skill as a draftsman and as a painter in oils.

What's the story?

Albrecht Dürer helped to transform the status of the artist from artisan to wealthy professional who commanded a workshop of assistants and whose patrons (customers) included kings and emperors. Dürer was filled with curiosity and this is reflected in the incredible diversity of his work, which covered everything from engravings to altarpieces, nature studies, landscapes, portraits, and works on the proportions of the human body.

Born in 1471, Dürer's father was a goldsmith and Dürer was trained in woodcutting and printing. Dürer was a supreme draftsman and it is this skill that shines out in *Portrait of Bernhard von Reesen*—every line counts, nothing is superfluous. Dürer settled in Nuremberg, Germany, where he opened a workshop staffed with assistants so that he could cope with the huge number of commissions he received. While working on these commissions Dürer perfected his technique of working in oil paints and this is possibly the greatest strength of the *Portrait of Bernhard von Reesen*. Dürer painted Bernhard's clothes with bold dynamic brushstrokes, saving all the fine detail for his face, which is framed by his hat and its shadow. Dürer recorded in his diary that "he made a portrait of Bernhart von Resten in oils" for which he was paid 8 florins. Sadly, Bernhard died only eight months later of the plague.

Portrait of Bernhard von Reesen	
Artist	Albrecht Dürer
Nationality	German
Painted	1521

Think about. . .

Why did Dürer paint this portrait mostly in black and white?
By using a limited range of colors our attention is focused on the sitter's face which, by contrast, is drawn in great detail. The use of just black and white also indicates that Bernhard is a serious and learned person, something that is emphasized further by the letter that Bernhard holds in his hand—during this time only members of the Church and rich people were able to read and write.

Project **Three-dimensional portrait**

This project concentrates on the line of a portrait rather than its color. Using PVA glue you can make a three-dimensional, raised image. Then you can paint it gold and rub it with black shoe polish to create an antique look.

1 Lightly draw or trace Dürer's portrait of Bernhard onto your white card. If you can't see through the card then use tracing paper or greaseproof paper to trace the image (see Top Tip). When you are happy with your drawing go over it neatly and clearly with your pencil.

2 Test your glue on a spare piece of paper to check that it's running smoothly and evenly. Carefully go over your pencil lines with the glue until all the pencil lines have been covered. Be careful to lift your glue up quickly when you have completed a line to avoid any drips.

You will need

A pencil

A sheet of thick white card or thick paper and a piece of cardboard glued together

Tracing paper or greaseproof paper

PVA glue in a container with a nozzle top

Spare scrap paper

Gold acrylic paint or poster paint

A medium-sized paintbrush

Black shoe polish

Soft cloth

3 At this point you might want to add some extra details like the folds of the shirt or curls of the hair. Let the glue dry overnight and then paint all over the picture with the gold paint.

4 When the gold paint is dry put some black shoe polish on a soft cloth and rub it all over the picture to give it an antique look.

Top tips

Here's how to transfer an image using tracing paper:

• Trace the image you want to copy using a pencil and some tracing paper or greaseproof baking paper.

• Flip the tracing paper and go over the lines of the portrait on the other side with your pencil.

• Turn the tracing paper back over again and put it on the card or paper you want to transfer the image to.

• Go over the lines of the portrait one more time—this will transfer the image.

Project **Rubber-band printing**

This activity uses rubber bands to create a simple printing technique. This project gets its inspiration from the fact that Albrecht Dürer was an engraver.

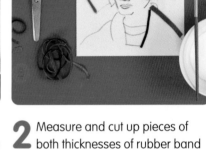

1 Start by drawing your portrait onto the cardboard (see Top Tip on page 41). You can use either Dürer's portrait on page 39 or your own design. Go over your pencil drawing with a ballpoint pen then apply a generous layer of PVA glue with the brush.

2 Measure and cut up pieces of both thicknesses of rubber band to fit over the lines of your drawing. Make sure the rubber is securely stuck onto the cardboard and leave it to dry.

3 Using your brush, put some white paint onto your sponge cloth.

4 Press the cardboard picture onto the white paint (rubber-band-side down) and press all across the back. Lift off your picture and place it face-up onto a folded newspaper. Choose a tissue square and put it on top of the cardboard. Press lightly. Lift off gently.

You will need

A square sheet of medium-thickness cardboard, 6 x 6in (15 x 15cm)

A pencil

Tracing paper

A ballpoint pen

PVA glue

A medium-sized paintbrush

Thick and thin rubber bands

A pair of scissors

A sponge cloth

White ready-mixed paint or poster paint

A newspaper

A sheet of white heavy paper—the size will depend on how many you make

Tissue paper, different colors, cut into squares 6 x 6in (15 x 15cm)

Glue stick or paper glue

5 Repeat step 4 again and again using different colors of tissue. Keep repeating this step until you have enough prints to fill your sheet of heavy paper.

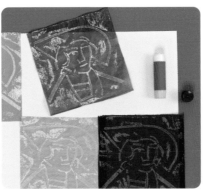

6 When the squares of tissue are dry, Using the glue stick, stick them down onto the heavy paper to create a checkerboard effect.

Top tips

• Wash your brush straight away after using the PVA glue.
• Once you have put the paint onto the sponge cloth work quickly before the paint dries.
• You could try using black or different colored paints for the prints instead of white.

Dream of America

If you had to choose an animal to represent America then it would have to be the buffalo—it reminds us of the wide, open spaces of the great American plains and the ancestry of the American plains Indians. In its strength and size, the buffalo represents a country that through its pioneering spirit has become the most powerful in the world. Yet in many ways this engraving of a buffalo makes many references to European art.

What's the story?

Jakob van der Schley was not a major artist but I have chosen to feature his work because his art tells us a lot about his time. For centuries most art in Europe was specially commissioned by a wealthy customer, called a patron, but during the eighteenth century the rising merchant classes wanted to show off their new wealth and education and they did so by buying art and books lavishly illustrated with engravings.

Engraving was a popular process because it allowed images to be copied in fine detail and then reproduced in large numbers. As Europeans went to explore the New World there was a huge demand for pictures of what they had seen there. Van der Schley responded with his engravings of animals, such as the buffalo. But if you look at the countryside in this engraving it looks more like a Dutch landscape than the American plains. Similarly, the buffalo resembles a minotaur, the monster of Greek legend. Having a Classical education (knowledge of Greek and Roman art and literature) was essential for every gentleman so someone who bought a van der Schley engraving was showing that they were a person of taste. Although *Buffel, Buffle* is an image of the New World it is also reassuringly European.

Buffel, Buffle	
Artist	Jakob van der Schley
Nationality	Dutch
Painted	*c.*1770

Think about. . .

Why did van der Schley choose to depict a buffalo in his engraving?
The buffalo represents the New World, as America was called then. Europeans were eager to learn about these newly-discovered lands and their plants and animals.

Who do you think would buy an engraving by van der Schley?
The new moneyed classes bought engravings—they had made their fortunes through trade and industry and were keen to show off their wealth and status. To show themselves as men of learning their libraries would house images of the New World.

BUFFLE.

BUFFEL.

"The buffalo looks like it's dancing."

Noah, age 6

Project **Cave painting**

This activity draws its inspiration from prehistoric cave paintings—a buffalo would be a very typical subject for such a painting. But relax, you don't have to find some suitable prehistoric cave to do this project, just grab some spackling plaster and paint.

1 Start by mixing up the spackling plaster. Mix up enough to fill the tray and then set it aside for a couple of hours, until it's hard.

2 Mix up your paint for the background. Brown earth tones would be appropriate. Apply the paint to the dry plaster and allow to dry.

You will need

A styrofoam tray (the type of tray that meat comes in), any size

Enough spackling plaster to fill the tray

Poster, watercolor, or powder paints

A medium-sized paintbrush

Rough sketch paper

A pencil

A thin paintbrush

A sheet of fine sandpaper

Watered-down PVA glue or a beaten egg (optional)

A thick paintbrush

3 Take your pencil and do a practice sketch of your buffalo (trace the outline of van der Schley's engraving on page 45 or draw a buffalo of your own). Lightly draw in any other background details, such as trees.

4 Now draw your buffalo design in pencil onto the painted spackling plaster. Paint-in the buffalo and any other details you want to include. Allow to dry.

5 Take your sandpaper and lightly sand over the painting to give it an aged appearance.

6 You might want to glaze the painting—this will add a sheen to the painting and help to protect it. You can make a glaze by using watered-down PVA glue or a beaten egg. Apply either substance with a brush and allow to dry. Remove the styrofoam tray and display your cave painting.

Top tips

- Take time when mixing up your colors to create rich earth tones.
- Make sure that the buffalo stands out against the background and does not blend in too much.
- For this project I prefer to use watercolor or powder paints because they can give a great variety of color tones.

Project **Buffalo painting**

This art project relates to the tribes of the North American plains Indians. The buffalo was integral to these peoples way of life. We are going to use fabric stained to imitate the color of buffalo hide. We will use a wooden frame as a reference to the way buffalo hides would have been stretched out to dry.

1 Ask an adult to make a pot of tea. When the tea has cooled pour it into a container. Scrunch up your fabric and soak it in the tea for a couple of hours. Remove the fabric from the tea and allow it to dry.

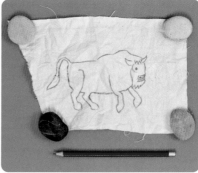

2 Stretch out the fabric and weigh down the corners. Sketch out your buffalo in pencil. You could trace van der Schley's engraving on page 45 or you can do your own drawing.

Top tips

• Don't choose yarn that is too fat or you won't be able to get it through the eye of the needle.
• Remember to secure the wool at the end.
• Remember to choose earth colors for your leaf prints.

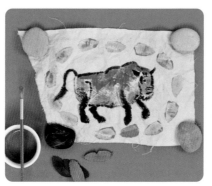

3 Paint in your buffalo and allow it to dry. Take a leaf and paint it using your chosen color. To ensure you have an even coverage of paint, do a test print on a bit of scrap paper. Press the leaf down and then lift it from the paper. Make a border of leaf prints around the buffalo and allow the paint to dry.

4 Thread and knot a length of yarn then sew a border using an over stitch. Not only is this sewing decorative but it prevents the fabric from fraying.

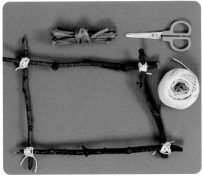

5 Make the frame with the sticks, overlapping them at the corners. Secure each corner with string. Once the frame is secure you may want to cover the string using raffia to give it a more natural look.

6 Cut four lengths of yarn, each about 16in (40cm) long. These are your corner ties. Thread a length and sew it into the corner of the fabric, then cut away so that you have two lengths for tying. Repeat at each of the other corners. Tie and secure each corner onto the frame. Your picture is now ready to be displayed.

You will need

A piece of cotton or muslin cloth, 8½ x 11in (A4) in size

Teabags

A plastic container

A pencil

Poster paints in earth tones

A variety of leaves for printing

Thin yarn

One large-eyed needle

Four sticks, two about 16in (40cm) in length and two about 8in (20cm) in length

String

Scissors

Raffia (optional)

3 Shape

No one would argue with the fact that shapes do not change their properties. A square will always have four equal sides, a triangle will have three sides of equal or unequal length. But as the next selection of paintings demonstrate (all produced within five years of each other), pictures may have a common theme but they can look startlingly different. To see what I mean, take a look at Juan Gris' vibrant *Nature Morte; violin et verre*, Theo van Doesburg's simple tonal *Composition*, and Kazimir Malevich's hard-edged *Suprematist Composition*.

Cube pictures

If you compare the paintings of Juan Gris (opposite) and Theo van Doesburg (look at page 59) they appear, at first glance, to be trying to express the same things in the same ways—they both feature architectural elements based on math. But while their starting point may have been the same, their end results are entirely different. Gris spoke of wanting to humanize abstract art, so in contrast to van Doesburg's very constructed, monotone paintings Gris' painting bursts with vibrant colors in a quirky still life, and his different textures and patterns create a highly decorative surface.

What's the story?

Juan Gris studied math, physics and engineering before taking up painting. By 1912 he was exhibiting paintings in the Cubist style. In Cubist paintings everyday objects were broken down into basic shapes, taken apart, and put back together again in a slightly disjointed way.

In 1912 Gris introduced the powerful element of color into his work and then he became expert in the second phase of Cubism, called Synthetic Cubism. Synthetic Cubism incorporated bits of newspaper, fabric, sheet music, magazines, and books, called *papier collé* ("pasted paper" in French) into pictures. Synthetic Cubism stuck objects together, rather than pulled them apart. We can see this quite clearly in *Nature Morte; violon et vere* (*Still Life; violin and glass*) where torn paper layers of lilac, pink tones, and ultramarine blue are set at angles to form the framework of the painting. The violin itself is fragmented into sections. Curling movement can be seen in the scroll of the violin and in the glass in a wonderfully rich, dense green, which is all the more startling set against the blue tones. Everywhere you look the swirling shapes create a dynamism like the rhythm of music itself.

Nature Morte; violon et vere	
Artist	Juan Gris
Nationality	Spanish
Painted	1913

Think about. . .

Unlike some Cubist artists, Gris used very strong vibrant colors. Was there a reason for this?
Gris' early paintings were monotone then, in 1912, influenced by Henri Matisse (see page 12) and a wishing to develop his own style, he started using color which added another new dimension to his paintings.

Why did Gris choose to paint a violin and a glass?
Cubist artists used everyday objects in their still life compositions. Gris painted several pictures that included a violin. His intention was to look at objects with fresh eyes.

"It looks like a jigsaw puzzle of a river."

Robin, aged 7

Project **Three-dimensional theme box**

This art project takes the idea of Juan Gris' painting—a collection of objects displayed—and reproduces it in a three-dimensional format. You can have fun finding objects with a linking theme if you want.

1 Start by taking your cardboard strips and painting them black. Set aside to dry.

2 While the strips are drying take your assortment of wrapping paper and tear it into random-sized pieces. Tear up enough pieces to line the inside of the box.

Top tips

• For the background paper choose colors that contrast with the objects you have collected. A contrasting color will help the objects to stand out.
• To make your display more interesting, make the compartments different sizes.
• If some of the objects you have chosen won't stay in place, use some Sticky Tack or double-sided tape to fix them into position.

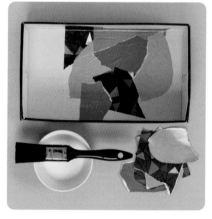

3 Like fitting pieces in a jigsaw together, glue down the pieces of paper to the inside of the box. Make sure that there are no gaps between the pieces of paper.

4 Take your cardboard strips and use them to divide your box into small compartments. The size and number of compartments will depend upon how many objects you have collected.

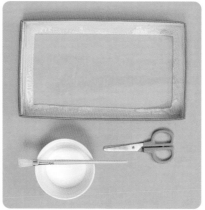

5 Glue your cardboard strips into place and allow them to dry and set. Arrange your objects in the compartments and glue them in place when you are happy with your arrangement.

6 Cut the center out of the shoebox lid, leaving a 1-in (2.5-cm) border all round. Measure up the transparent plastic so that it will fit inside the box lid then stick it in place, making sure that you have an even overlap on all sides.

You will need

PVA glue

Black poster paint

A paintbrush

Strips of strong cardboard long enough to fit the box

An assortment of wrapping paper or wallpaper

A shoebox with a lid

A collection of small objects with a theme such as nature, e.g. pine cones, feathers, leaves, bark etc.

A pair of scissors

Transparent plastic large enough to cover the box lid

Project **Cubist photographs**

This art project borrows the Cubist style of disjointed
images but with a modern twist—by using photographic
images that have been cut up and reassembled.

A selection of magazines or a digital camera

A pair of scissors

Glue stick or paper glue

Some poster or watercolor paints

A paintbrush

A pencil

A sheet of 11 x 17in (A3) white heavy paper or any size

1 Decide the theme of your picture. Here are some examples; music, water, nature, or time. Using some magazines, cut out and collect images to do with the theme you have chosen. If you can't find pictures of the images you want, see if you can take photos of them instead and then print them out.

2 Now decide on a suitable setting for your cut-out images. What kind of table or surface should they be on? Then decide on a background. Try to include different patterns, textures, and background colors. Sketch out the setting. Now paint in the background and foreground. Allow to dry.

3 Cut the images up into pieces. Arrange the images onto the painted sheet. Set them at an angle, slightly disjointed.

4 When you are happy with your arrangement, glue the pieces down into their final positions.

Top tips

Take time to cut out and select your images and also take time to create the best arrangement.

Building blocks

In Theo van Doesburg's painting *Composition*, sometimes called *Ragtime*, there are no figures, no story, no colors, just tones of gray and an arrangement of shapes. Yet this image catches our attention, making us think and reflect.

What's the story?

Theo van Doesburg joined a group of young Dutch artists to produce a journal in 1917 called *De Stijl* (meaning "the style"). In this journal they set out their ideas on art and De Stijl also became the name of their art movement, although it is also known as Neo-Plasticism. De Stijl paintings featured horizontal and vertical lines and used black, white, and primary colors. De Stijl artists thought that art should be represented in as exact a way as math. De Stijl ideas also applied to architecture, furniture, and decorative objects like plates and fabrics.

For Van Doesburg the De Stijl movement was also about changing the role of the artist in society and he thought that architecture should play an important part in achieving this. You only have to look at *Composition* to see the link van Doesburg made between art and architecture because the picture appears to be constructed of building blocks. The way van Doesburg shaded the painting in tones of gray created drama in the picture. Every time I look at this painting it suggests different things to me; the stones of an ancient culture, doorways opening onto unknown paths, and, in the sections of circles and ovals, a piece of the Milky Way.

The painting's alternative title, *Ragtime*, suggests a further link between Neo-Plasticism and math. Music, like math, follows a strict beat and pattern. Whistler (page 32) also saw a link between art and music and van Doesburg's work is almost the next step in Whistler's theories on art.

Composition	
Artist	Theo van Doesburg
Nationality	Dutch
Painted	1918

Think about. . .

Why did van Doesburg choose not to use any color in his painting?
Van Doesburg felt that using color would detract from the beauty of the shapes. He used tones of gray to bring out the form of the shapes and to give them a structural, three-dimensional quality.

Why did van Doesburg give the painting the alternative title of *Ragtime*?
Music, like math, has a regular time and beat so van Doesburg was stressing the ordered nature of his painting by naming it after a type of jazz music.

Project **Dramatic sculpture**

This project turns van Doesburg's *Composition* into a three-dimensional sculpture and uses a task lamp to add dramatic light and shadow effects.

1 Start by arranging and assembling your containers into a shape. When you are happy with your arrangement, glue together the pieces. Allow the glue to dry and set—this can take several hours.

You will need

Small empty containers like matchboxes, plastic cups, and paper towels tubes

PVA glue

White acrylic paint

A large paintbrush

A task lamp or a flashlight

Black acrylic paint

A medium paintbrush

An old plate for mixing the paint

2 Paint your sculpture all over in white acrylic paint. You might need to do more than one coat, the main thing to do is to cover up any signs of the packaging beneath.

3 After the white paint has dried, take the task lamp and shine it onto your sculpture. If you are using a torch it might be a good idea to rest it on some books. The shadows should be very clear. Find the darkest shadow and try to match its color by mixing up your paint to that shade. Apply the paint to those areas. Now find the next lightest tone, mixing your paint to match the tone and adding it to the sculpture. Keep repeating this step until all the tones of the shadows have been painted in. Now display your sculpture.

Top tips

- Be inventive with the way you arrange your containers, don't just line them up, face-on, but put them at odd angles or cut up the tubes and place them sideways so that you can see the circles they make.
- You may want to use more than one light or torch to create more dramatic light effects.
- Take time to mix up the correct color shades—it really helps to create the final effect.

Project Weaving with paper

This art project captures the sculptural, three-dimensional quality of van Doesburg's painting by making a paper loom using corrugated cardboard. The corrugated paper has a textured, raised surface which creates it's own sense of movement, light and shade. The loom is woven with paper strips in different shades of gray.

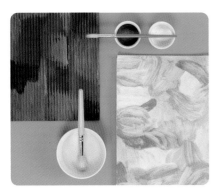

1 Start by making the heavy paper wet with your big paintbrush. While the paper is still wet, cover the surface in shades of gray. Leave the painted paper to dry. Do the same with the corrugated paper but do not wet the paper first. Allow this to dry.

2 Measure and mark off a 1½-in (4-cm) border around the corrugated cardboard. Then measure and mark off vertical strips every ½in (1.25cm) from the top of the border to the bottom. Starting at the top, cut along the marked out lines, stop when you get to the bottom border.

You will need

A sheet of 8½ x 11in (A4) white heavy paper

Paintbrushes, thick and thin

Black and white poster paints or watercolor paint

A sheet of corrugated cardobard, 8½ x 11in (A4) or larger

A ruler

A white pencil

A pair of scissors

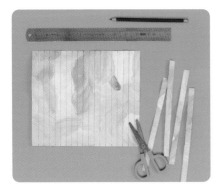

3 Measure and mark off ½-in (1.25-cm) horizontal lines on the heavy paper then cut into strips.

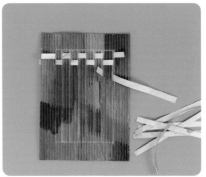

4 Take a cut strip and, in an over-and-under action, weave through the corrugated paper. Keep repeating this with new strips until you reach the bottom. Adjust strips so that they are even on both sides and there are no gaps between the strips.

Top tips

• As you are weaving you may need to nudge the paper strips down to fill in any gaps.
• Make sure that you stick to the over-and-under action and remember not to skip over more than one vertical section.

Shapes in space

Kazimir Malevich's art propels us into the world of twentieth-century painting with a force that is breathtaking in its inventiveness. In Malevich's pictures all references to the history of painting have been swept away. Every element of Malevich's paintings are pared down in order to announce the arrival of the new age of industrialism and technology.

What's the story?

Kazimir Malevich was born in Kiev (modern-day Ukraine) in 1878. He studied at the Moscow Institute of Painting, Sculpture and Architecture from 1904–10. After 1910 his painting changed and developed into the style that became known as Suprematism. Suprematism was a version of Cubism. In Cubist paintings everyday objects were broken down into basic shapes, taken apart, and put back together again in a slightly disjointed way. Malevich showed his geometric Suprematist paintings to the public in Petrograd, Russia, in 1915. In these paintings he tried to make geometric shapes represent feelings or sensations. He also looked at developing the Suprematist style in three-dimensional models of buildings and this is very obvious when we look at this painting—the geometric shapes have a sculptural feel, as if you could reach out and grab hold of them. The sharp-edged, flat shapes seem to be welded together. He used bold primary colors and black to add to the painting's hard-edged atmosphere. The whole composition is made up of straight lines. Yet, despite the solid quality of the central shapes, the thin slivers of rectangles seem to fly away at random; this creates a feeling of movement so that the whole structure looks like a plane about to take off.

Suprematist Composition	
Artist	Kazimir Malevich
Nationality	Russian
Painted	1915

Think about. . .

If different colors had been used in the picture would it have mattered?
Cover up the black and see how this changes the painting. The green and black in the middle of the picture weigh down the large shapes there. If you painted these three shapes in light colors they would look as though they were floating away, not anchored down.

What would happen if you put circles into this painting?
The picture would look less rigid and the structural feel of the image would be lost.

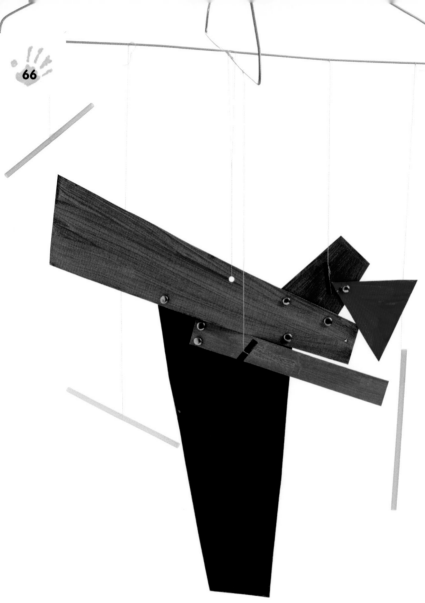

1 Start by tracing the outlines of the shapes in the painting (page 65) onto your cardboard. Cut out the cardboard shapes and paint them on one side. When the painted side is dry paint the other side.

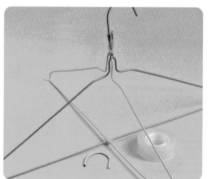

Project **Mobile sculpture**

How can we recreate the sculptural feel of Malevich's painting? How can we recreate Malevich's floating shapes? The answer is to make a three-dimensional hanging mobile sculpture.

4 Take one of the coat hangers and get an adult to cut away the hook with the pliers. Now insert one hanger through the other at a right angle to form a cross. Tape the hangers together at the point where they meet along the bottom and at the top, below the hook.

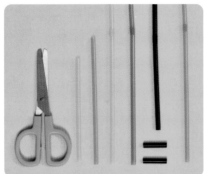

You will need

A large piece of thick cardboard, an old supermarket box or shoebox is ideal

A piece of tracing paper or greaseproof paper

A pencil

A pair of scissors

Poster or acrylic paints in the same colors as the painting or your own choice

A medium-sized paintbrush

Six split pins

About six brightly-colored straws

Two wire coat hangers (triangular in shape)

Pliers

Sticky tape

Cotton thread

2 Assemble the pieces and mark with a pencil where you need an adult to make the holes for the split pins. Pin the shapes together and make a hole in the biggest card shape (the green section). This is where your sculpture will hang from.

3 Now cut the straws into a variety of different lengths.

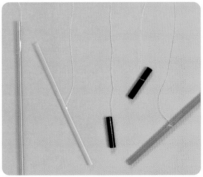

5 Attach some cotton thread (about 8in [20cm] long) to the biggest cardboard section through the pre-made hole. Now tie the thread to the crossbar of the hangers.

6 Cut threads between 8in (20cm) and 16in (40cm) long to match the number of straws. Tape a length of thread onto each straw so that some of the straws will hang vertically and some horizontally. Tie the straws along the crossbars of the hangers. Now you can hang up your mobile.

Project **Color blending**

This art activity recreates the light, floating quality of the color blocks in Malevich's painting by using paint on wet paper—this makes the colors run and blend together.

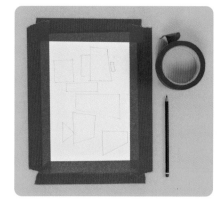

1 Start by sticking your paper onto your board or onto a clean table top with the masking tape. If you are using a table top make sure that the tape will not leave a mark when it is removed. Lightly sketch in where you want your blocks of color to go.

2 Wet your sponge and wring out any extra water then drag the sponge across the paper in broad horizontal strokes so that the whole page becomes wet.

You will need

A sheet of 8½ x 11in (A4) or larger white watercolor paper or heavy paper

A board larger than the paper, or a clean table top

Masking tape

A pencil

A sponge

Watercolor paints or powder paints

A thin- to medium-sized paintbrush

3 Now start filling in the blocks of color remembering to clean your brush every time you use a new color.

4 When the paper and paint are dry take the paper off the board or table top. You may like to go on to do a series of these paintings using a different combination of colors within the same shapes for each one.

4 Animals

Animals are possibly one of the most popular subjects in art, from the earliest cave paintings of prehistory right through to the present day. Animals have been recorded in every type of medium, in sculpture, on canvas, in wood, on ceramics, and in tapestries. The paintings and activities in this chapter reflect this breadth and diversity of subject matter and medium. Included here are Rousseau's iconic *Surprised!*, Jacopo Zucchi's enchanting fresco *Pergola with Birds*, and George Stubbs' masterful *A Couple of Fox Hounds*.

A tiger's view of the jungle

Think of all the pictures that have been painted of animals and *Surprised!*, Henri Rousseau's painting of a tiger in a storm, is surely one of the most popular. What's the secret of the painting's enduring appeal? I think the answer is that if you had never seen a photograph of a jungle, this is probably how you would hope it would look—an exotic location, a dramatic storm, and of course a tiger. All these elements are combined in a powerful and bold way to create an image that once seen is never forgotten.

What's the story?

Rousseau claimed that he had experience of the jungle from his time as a regimental guardsman in Mexico with the French Army but when he was in the army he never left France. His jungle picture was created from plant studies he made at the botanical gardens, prints by other artists, and his imagination.

Rousseau had no art training and he painted the jungle with a simple, naïve quality. But this style adds to the drama, giving the picture a raw, direct energy.

Rousseau saw the jungle as if through a child's eye. Great big green glossy leaves frame the crouching tiger, who is ready to spring. For the final touch of drama a streak of lightning cuts through the dark storm clouds. The drama and emotion of the scene is heightened because there appears to be a conflict between nature and the tiger. The tiger digs in his claws to maintain his position against the full force of the wind. His body position tells us that he senses the danger but refuses to be cowed by it and, in a final act of defiance, he bares his teeth at the flash of lightning. Maybe it is this aspect of the painting that appeals most to people—the tiger standing firm against the odds.

Surprised!	
Artist	Henri Rousseau
Nationality	French
Painted	1891

Think about. . .

How did Rousseau manage to get such a sense of movement into the picture?
By painting all the trees and plants of the jungle in strong diagonals from left to right. The tiger's body is also a diagonal but it is rigid with his claws dug in to maintain his position against the wind—reinforcing the obvious strength of the storm.

How important is the lightning?
It adds to the tension and drama of the scence, highlighting the force of the storm. Apart from the tiger's teeth, the lightning is the only place where white paint has been used.

"The tiger looks really scared—I'd help him out of the forest."

Holly, age 6

Project **Jungle box**

With nothing more than an old shoebox, this activity recreates Rousseau's *Surprised!* in a three-dimensional format. The shoebox works on the same principal as a pinhole camera and gives you a clearer understanding of how objects can look small or large depending on their distance from the viewer.

1 Cut out the top of the box lid in a rectangular shape, leaving a border of about 1in (2.5cm).

4 When the paint is dry arrange the soil, pebbles, and plants inside the box, weighing them down with Sticky Tack.

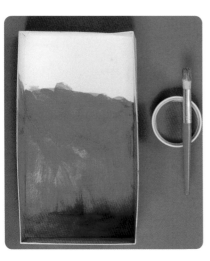

2 Paint the inside of the box. While the paint is drying, measure up a piece of tissue paper to fit the box lid.

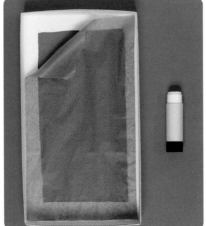

3 Glue the border inside the box lid and stick down the prepared tissue paper.

5 Make a small peep hole at one end of the box with the point of your scissors. Paint a streak of lightning at the other end of the box on the inside.

6 Place the tiger in your jungle scene and put the lid on the box. View the scene through the hole. Experiment with the position of the tiger to see how it affects the image.

You will need

A shoebox, with lid, of any size

A pair of scissors

Green paint—enough to paint the inside of the box

A medium-sized paintbrush

Green tissue paper— enough to cover the lid of the box

A glue stick or paper glue

Two or three handfuls of soil

Between five and ten small pebbles or rocks

Small pieces of plants

Sticky tack

White paint

A thin paintbrush

One plastic tiger

Project **Three-dimensional collage**

This art project is a collage made up of printed cut-outs made out of a variety of materials. The collage technique gives the picture a dynamic, three-dimensional appearance.

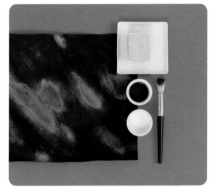

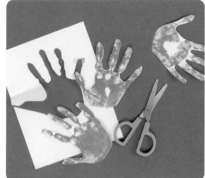

1 Wet the black paper all over with the sponge. Now paint in the stormy sky, covering the page with slanting diagonal strokes to create the effect of the rain. Let the paper dry.

2 Make handprints with the green poster paint on one of your sheets of white paper. The number you will need will depend on the size of the piece of black paper you are using. When the handprints are dry, carefully cut them out.

You will need

A sheet of strong black paper,

A sponge

A medium-sized paintbrush

Poster paints in a variety of colors

A plate for mixing paints

About three sheets of white paper, any size

A pair of scissors

A selection of leaves

Pieces of broccoli

A thin paintbrush

A glue stick or paper glue

3 On a clean sheet of paper make prints of the leaves in a red-orange color. Cut the broccoli in half and repeat the printing process with the broccoli in a contrasting color.

4 On a separate sheet of paper sketch out a tiger or trace Rousseau's tiger on page 73. Paint the tiger and allow it to dry. Cut out the tiger and the leaf and broccoli prints when they are dry.

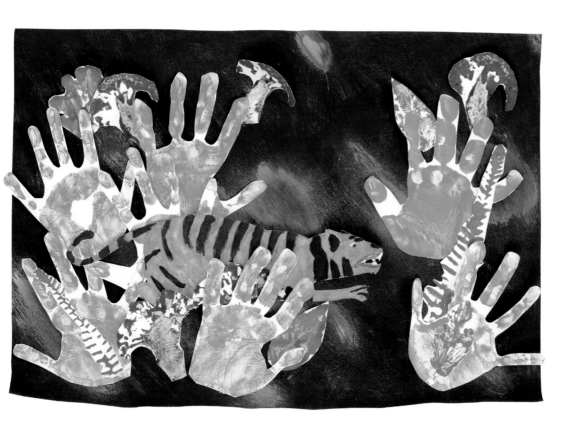

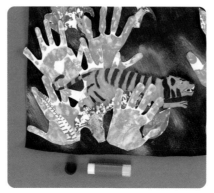

5 Arrange the prints on the paper with the broccoli representing the trees and the leaves and hands representing the plants and grasses.

6 Place the tiger in amongst your cut-out prints. Glue down all the pieces of paper when you are happy with your composition.

Top tips

• Clean your hands between using the different paint colors.
• Don't glue down the prints completely—leaving them free at the edges will give a more three-dimensional effect.

Exotic birds

Every artist leaves a bit of their personality in the works they create but Jacopo Zucchi's *Pergola with Birds* tells us as much about Ferdinando de' Medici—the person who commissioned the work—as the artist. This fresco was meant to impress visitors to Ferdinando's pavilion in Rome, with its stunning optical illusion and exotic birds.

What's the story?

As the Grand Duke of Tuscany Ferdinando was the head of the Medici family, who had become very wealthy through their banking business. They became patrons of the arts, employing artists such as Michelangelo. They saw art as a way not only to beautify their palaces but also as a tool to enhance their power and fame.

Jacopo del Zucchi was born in Italy in 1540 and was trained as a painter by the influential artist and writer Giorgio Vasari. In 1572 Zucchi moved to Rome where he became artist-in-residence (live-in artist) to the Medici court. When he was living in Rome Zucchi was influenced by the Mannerist style of painting that he saw in the work of artists such as Raphael and Michelangelo. Mannerist artists elongated the length of people's arms, legs, and necks in order to change body shapes to suit their ideas of physical beauty. Mannerism can look quite artificial, rather than natural. In Zucchi's pergola fresco you can see a combination of the different artistic influences he had encountered. In the ornate structure of the pergola you can see the use of mathematical perspective, something that had been perfected in Florence, used here to create an illusion of space, height, and depth so that the viewer feels as though they have just walked straight into the pergola. The theatrical presentation and rich, opulent colors in Zucchi's pergola reflect the influence of the Mannerist style of painting.

Pergola with Birds

Artist	Jacopo Zucchi
Nationality	Italian
Painted	1576–1577

Think about. . .

What is a pavilion?
A pavilion is a building erected near a person's main house that is used for entertainment outdoors. Pavilions reflected the high status of their owners.

What is a pergola?
A framework for climbing plants.

How does the way the foliage is painted add to the illusion of being inside the pergola?
The branches of the trees appear to intertwine with the structure of the pergola and the top-most branches give the impression of hanging over the top of the dome to give an even greater feeling of height and space.

Project **Bird tapestry**

In this simple weaving project wools and fabrics are used to create a sky backdrop on which birds are placed to make it appear three-dimensional. Wealthy Europeans in the sixteenth century thought that tapestries and wall hangings were beautiful works of art that were also practical—they helped to block out drafts—and they were also a way of showing the owner's wealth and status.

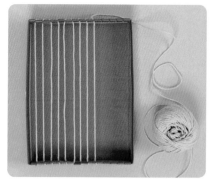

1 Cut into the box at ½-inch intervals, a ½in (1.25cm) deep at the top and bottom of the inside of the box lid. Tape a long piece of yarn or string to the outside of the lid and then wrap around vertically inside, using the cuts to hold the string in place. Your final end of string should finish where you started. For extra strength tie these two ends together and tape down. These are called warp threads.

4 Cut away the warp strings of yarn at the back of the lid to detach your weaving from the lid.

You will need

One shoebox lid, any size

A ball of string

A pair of scissors

A selection of yarn in different shades of blue

A sheet of 8½ x 11in (A4) white posterboard or heavy paper

A pencil

Felt-tip pens or colored pencils

Double-sided tape

2 Choose a color of yarn and tie the end to the furthest right-hand yarn warp. Now begin weaving over and under the warps. When you reach the end come back again, weaving all the way. These horizontal yarn threads are called the wefts. Weave a section about an inch wide. When you have completed one shade of blue, tie it off and weave another shade of blue, then another, and so on until the end.

3 On your sheet of heavy paper draw pictures of birds. You can do your own designs or copy the ones in Zucchi's fresco. Color in the birds and then cut them out.

Top tips

• Make sure that your vertical strands of string are tight otherwise the horizontal strands of yarn will not hold.

• After you complete each shade of blue, gently push up the weft threads so that the weave is tight.

• You could add seeds, beads, or feathers to your birds.

• You can also weave with ribbons or fabric strips instead of yarn.

5 Your weaving will look like a little rug. Trim the yarn to make a fringe and make knots at the top of each warp to secure your weaving.

6 Arrange the paper birds on your tapestry. Use small pieces of double-sided tape to attach the birds to your weaving.

Project **Bird sculpture**

This modern sculpture project takes inspiration from the pergola itself. You will set cut-out drawings of birds on a curving sculpture of straws that has a feeling of movement and lightness.

1 Start by checking how many straws fit around your container, standing upright. Mix up the plaster of Paris with some water to make a thick paste. Put the paste in your container, leaving about an inch free at the top.

4 When the filler has set cut away the container. You may need an adult to help you with this.

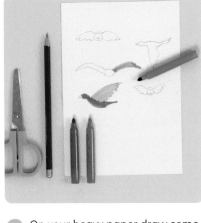

2 Now place your straws around the edge of the container, standing them upright in the plaster. Leave for a few hours so that the plaster sets hard.

3 On your heavy paper draw some birds. Use Zucchi's fresco on page 79 as inspiration. You will need to draw one bird for every two or three straws in your container. Color the birds in and then cut them out.

Use Zucchi's fresco on page 79 as inspiration.

You will need

A small plastic round container such as a mini ice cream tub

Plaster of Paris, enough to fill three-quarters of your container

A mixing bowl or container for the plaster

A handful of thick plastic straws

A sheet of 8½ x 11in (A4) heavy paper

A pencil

Colors—crayons, felt-tip pens, or colored pencils

A pair of scissors

A marker pen

Sticky tack or double-sided sticky tape

5 Mark the straws with your pen at regular intervals, like steps going down. The first straw does not need to be cut. Cut the rest of the straws, using your pen marks as a guide.

6 Attach your birds to the straws using Sticky Tack or double-sided sticky tape.

Top tip

Get your straws quickly into position once the plaster is in the container because it sets rapidly.

Perfect pets

If you are lucky enough to own a pet you will know that sometimes we begin to think that our pets have human qualities and characteristics. Looking at George Stubbs' *A Couple of Foxhounds* you might think that these dogs were someone's beloved pets—not just two dogs taken from a hunting pack. Stubbs was so skilled that he was able to convey the character of these dogs and the almost human relationship between them. We can admire Stubbs' skill as a draftsman and his sensitive use of oil paints, but it is his ability to depict the character of these dogs that makes this painting special.

A Couple of Foxhounds	
Artist	George Stubbs
Nationality	British
Painted	1792

What's the story?

Why was George Stubbs so good at painting animals? Probably because he knew his subjects inside-out—literally. Stubbs spent hours cutting open dead horses so that he could study how the muscles and skeleton looked and worked. His studies resulted in the publication in 1766 of *Anatomy of the Horse*, an illustrated book of his drawings and discoveries. This book brought him fame throughout Europe, not only because horses were the main method of transport so many people had one, but because people recognized the quality and skill of his work. Wealthy people rushed to have their prize horses and animals painted by Stubbs.

Despite Stubbs' intense interest in his subject, he looked at whatever he was painting with cool detachment, setting the animals or figures in a perfectly composed natural-looking landscape. *A Couple of Foxhounds* was painted late in Stubbs' career as an artist and it brings together all the skills he had learned over all the years he had been painting. In it he demonstrates that he was one of the greatest artists of the eighteenth century.

Think about. . .

Why did Stubbs choose to show an imaginary landscape rather than a real one?
Stubbs wanted to bring out the best in the dogs so he created a landscape which showed off their beauty.

How did Stubbs manage to show the close relationship between the dogs?
Stubbs displayed his skill as a draughtsman in his sensitive handling of the heads of the dogs—the position of their heads suggests a closeness and the male dog looks as though he is protecting the female.

"I think those dogs are friends. They might even be married."

Jill, age 6

Project **Wall plaque**

George Stubbs worked with the famous English potter Josiah Wedgwood. Stubbs painted a series of scenes of the countryside using delicate enamel colors on pottery plaques. This art activity uses the much simpler technique of painting on salt dough (Play-Doh).

1 Combine all the ingredients needed for the salt dough in the mixing bowl. Knead for ten minutes. Set aside in the fridge.

2 Trace around the dog shapes on page 85 or use your own designs. Cut out your trace of the dogs and transfer onto the cardboard or paper to make into stencils.

Top tip

• Increase the quantity of salt dough according to the size of plaque you want to create.
• Add a tablespoon of vegetable oil to the salt dough to make kneading easier.
• Add a tablespoon of lemon juice to make the dough set harder at the finished stage.

3 Lightly flour your work surface and roll out half of the salt dough to approximately 8 x 7 in (20 x 17.5cm). Use a ruler to help you get straight sides and the correct size.

4 Now roll out the remaining dough, making sure that it's big enough for the two stencils to fit. Take your pencil and mark around the stencils. Lift off the stencils and cut out the dog shapes. You may need some adult help for this stage.

5 With the help of an adult, place the dough pieces onto a non-stick baking tray and put in the oven at 125°F (50°C) for thirty minutes and then increase the temperature to 212°F (100°C) for 3½–4 hours. Turn the dough pieces during this drying stage. Allow the dough to cool in the oven.

6 Paint the dogs and background. When the paint is dry, glue the dogs onto the rectangular piece of salt dough and then apply a coat of slightly watered-down PVA glue to give a nice shiny finish to your work.

To make salt dough mix 2 cups (100g) of plain flour with 1 cup (250g) of salt and 1 cup (250ml) of water

Tracing paper

A pencil

Cardboard to make stencils

Flour for dusting

A rolling pin

A ruler

A knife to cut dough

A non-stick baking tray

Poster or watercolor paints

A paintbrush

PVA glue, watered down

Project Pebble paperweight

This activity is about making a pebble paperweight showing a dog. You could make more paperweights showing other animals that fit the space, such as a curled up cat.

Top tip

• When painting your dog, allow each color to dry before adding another. This way you will stop the colors from running into each other.
• If you have difficulty finding a large smooth pebble you could try going to a garden center or a hardware store to buy one.

You will need

A large pebble, approximately 4in (10cm) long, as smooth as possible

A selection of poster paints including black, brown, white, blue, and green

Medium-sized, thin, and thick paintbrushs

A pencil

Rough sketch paper

Enough PVA glue, watered down, to coat the pebble

1 Wash and dry the pebble so that it is clean. Do a sketch of a dog on the rough piece of paper. Paint the pebble a light blue color all over, and let it dry. Add a dark brown area at the bottom where the dog will stand. Let the paint dry.

2 Lightly sketch your dog onto the pebble.

3 Paint in your dog using the poster paints. Add any other background details you want.

4 When the paint is dry coat your pebble with a layer of slightly watered-down PVA glue and let it dry—the glue will become see-through when it is dry and will give the painted pebble a nice shine and a layer of protection.

Artist biographies

Theo van Doesburg

1883–1931

Dutch

Theo van Doesburg was a Dutch architect, poet, decorator, and painter who founded the De Stijl art movement in 1917. To begin with several artists, including Piet Mondrian (1872–1944) and Bart van der Leck (1876–1958), grouped together to publish a magazine that told people about their views on art; the magazine was called *De Stijl* ("the style" in Dutch) and soon the art movement itself was known by the same name. De Stijl artists believed that art was about more than representing the world around us—they thought that it should be a spiritual experience. De Stijl artists thought that the only way art could be spiritual was for it to mirror the harmony and order of math—so only squares, rectangles, and horizontal and vertical straight lines were used and only pure primary (red, yellow, and blue) colors and black and white were allowed. De Stijl artists wanted their paintings to be very disciplined. De Stijl art was abstract, which means it did not represent the world in a realistic way. Van Doesburg was the leading member of De Stijl and he traveled to Germany to visit the Bauhaus, the most influential art and design school in Europe at the time, to promote De Stijl's ideas.

Albrecht Dürer

1471–1528

German

Dürer was one of the most important artists in Western art thanks to the huge number of works he created, his thriving print business, which meant that his art was seen all over Europe, and his many skills and talents—he was a woodblock artist, an engraver, a painter, printmaker, and a writer on art, math, and perspective.

Juan Gris

1887–1927

Spanish

Juan Gris was a Cubist painter and sculptor who lived in France. Cubism was an art movement founded by Georges Braque (1882–1963) and Pablo Picasso (1881–1973). An art critic, Louis Vauxcelles, named the movement by noticing that Cubist pictures were "full of little cubes." The first phase of Cubism was called Analytical Cubism and it was active between 1908 and 1912. In Analytical Cubism paintings everyday objects were broken down into basic shapes, taken apart, and put back together again in a slightly disjointed way to represent an object from lots of different angles at the same time. The second phase of Cubism took place between 1912 and 1919 and was called Synthetic Cubism. Synthetic Cubism incorporated collage—bits of newspapers, fabric, sheet music, magazines, and books—into pictures. Synthetic Cubism stuck objects together, rather than pulled them apart. Juan Gris was involved in both kinds of Cubism but is better known for his Synthetic Cubism.

Lipunja

dates unknown

Aboriginal Australian

We know very little about Lipunja, other than the fact that this artist was working in Arnhem Land, Australia, in the 1960s.

Kazimir Malevich

1879–1935

Russian

Kazimir Malevich studied at the Moscow Institute of Painting, Sculpture, and Architecture from 1904–10. In 1913 Malevich saw Cubist works for the first time, was greatly influenced by them, and began painting in a Cubist style. In 1915 Malevich created his own style of art, which he called Suprematism. Suprematism was a truly Russian art movement and was based on geometric shapes, such as squares and circles, painted in starkly-contrasting colors, such as a black square floating on a white background, or a black circle floating on a white background.

Henri Matisse

1869–1954

French

Henri Matisse was a lawyer who turned to painting after his mother bought him a set of paints to amuse himself while recovering from appendicitis. Matisse went on to become one of the greatest artists of the twentieth century. Matisse was not only a painter, but also a sculptor and printmaker. He is best known for his bold and expressive use of bright colors and flowing drawing style. As a young man Matisse was a founding member of a group of artists called the *Fauves*, which means "wild beasts" in French. These artists used bright, unmixed colors in a bold and energetic style to express their emotions. One of Matisse's most famous Fauvist paintings is *Woman with a Hat* (1905). With time, Matisse became more and more respected, producing a great deal of work between 1906 and 1917 as part of the Paris avant-garde art scene.

After 1917 Matisse moved outside Paris and continued to create a vast quantity of work right up until his death in 1954 at the age of eighty-four.

Henri Rousseau

1844–1910

French

Henri Rousseau worked as a customs officer for most of his life and taught himself to paint. At the age of forty-nine he gave up his work and concentrated on painting. Rousseau's paintings are called naïve or primitive because they seem quite child-like but they are actually very complex and skilled. Rousseau's landscapes have a magical atmosphere, possibly because he made a lot of his pictures up—he painted pictures of jungles but he had never been to a jungle. Rousseau didn't receive approval from art critics during his lifetime but he influenced the next generation of artists, including Pablo Picasso.

Jakob van der Schley

1715–1779

Dutch

Jakob van der Schley was born in 1715 and was trained by Bernard Picart. He worked in Amsterdam and St. Petersburg, mainly as an engraver.

Georges Seurat

1859–1891

French

Georges Seurat invented a new style of painting called Pointillism, or Divisionism, where tiny dots of color are painted next to each other which, from a distance, take on the appearance of different colors. Seurat based his painting style on scientific color theories that were popular at the time. He painted *A Sunday Afternoon on the Island of La Grande Jatte*, (1884–6), in his Pointillist style—it measures 10ft (3m) across and took him two years to complete—it has become one of the most famous pictures of the twentieth century. *A Sunday Afternoon on the Island of La Grande Jatte* can be seen at the Art Institute of Chicago. Seurat died at the age of thirty-one.

George Stubbs

1724–1806

English

Stubbs was born in Liverpool, England. Between 1745 and 1751 he made a living painting portraits in the north of England and in his spare time he studied anatomy at York County hospital. Stubbs studied horses in great detail, spending eighteen months dissecting them and drawing every aspect of them. Stubbs' book, *The Anatomy of the Horse*, was published in 1766 and was an instant success. Stubbs was a meticulous artist, obsessed by understanding anatomy as a means of perfecting his art. Stubbs worked for wealthy people who kept horses and packs of hunting dogs and wanted a record of their ownership of the animals. Stubbs also painted lions, tigers, and monkeys.

James Abbott McNeill Whistler

1834–1903

American

Whistler was born in Lowell, Massachusetts, and attended West Point Military Academy. Whistler did not enjoy West Point. He grew his hair too long, was shabby on parade, and did not excel academically. He did, however, learn drawing and mapmaking from Robert W. Weir, the historical painter and a member of the Hudson River school of American art. After leaving West Point Whistler worked as a draftsman, drawing the U.S. coastline for the military. Whistler was bored with this work and drew mermaids and sea creatures in the spaces around the maps. In 1855 Whistler decided to become a painter and he traveled to Paris where he took a studio, studied art, got into debt, and met Edouard Manet (1832–83), Charles Baudelaire (1821–67), Gustave Courbet (1819–77), and Theophile Gautier (1811–72). In 1859 Whistler moved to London, which was to be his home for the rest of his life. Whistler now perfected his painting style, working on pictures with a limited range of colors so that his compositions had an overall tonal harmony. Whistler was attempting to paint the harmony that is present in music. Whistler was also influenced by the composition of Japanese prints. Whistler's most famous picture is *Arrangement in Gray and Black: The Artist's Mother*, also known as *Whistler's Mother,* and it can be seen in the Musée d'Orsay in Paris.

Jacopo Zucchi

1540–1596

Italian

Jacopo del Zucchi was an Italian artist from Florence who trained with Giorgio Vasari and assisted him in the decoration of the Palazzo Vecchio, Florence's town hall. Zucchi also worked for the powerful Medici family.

A

Abstract: A picture that doesn't look anything like objects, people, or things in the world. Many art movements of the twentieth century were abstract and a lot of today's art is abstract.

Artisan: A skilled workman or craftsman, such as a carpenter.

C

Chevreul, Michel Eugène: A chemist who had a keen interest in restoring tapestries. Chevreul noted that when he filled in a bare patch on a tapestry he had to take into consideration the color of the wool surrounding the bare patch. Chevreul discovered that if he sewed certain colors of wool right next to each other they looked like a different color from a distance. From these practical observations he formulated the color wheel, which shows the complementary color of every color at the opposite position on the wheel. Artists were very interested in Chevreul's theories and the Pointillists used his theories in their work.

Classical myths: Stories from the cultures of the ancient Greeks and Romans.

Composition: The arrangement of elements in a picture such as line, color, and form.

Courbet, Gustave (1819–1877): French painter and leader of the Realist movement. The Realists painted ordinary things—such as poverty, rural life, and working people—rather than the traditional subjects of the day, such as famous people, incidents from history, Classical mythology, and scenes from the Bible. The Realists painted in a rough style, applying the paint in a way that was meant to indicate that they had seen the thing they were depicting, rather than being restricted to working in a studio.

Cubism: An art critic, Louis Vauxcelles, named the Cubist movement by noticing that Cubist pictures were "full of little cubes." The first phase of Cubism was called Analytical Cubism and it was active between 1908 and 1912. In Analytical Cubism paintings' everyday objects were broken down into basic shapes, taken apart, and put back together again in a slightly disjointed way to represent an object from lots of different angles at the same time. The second phase of Cubism took place between 1912 and 1919 and was called Synthetic Cubism. Synthetic Cubism incorporated collage—bits of newspapers, fabric, sheet music, magazines, and books—into pictures. Synthetic Cubism stuck objects together, rather than pulled them apart.

D

De Stijl: Dutch for "The Style," was an art movement that originated in the Netherlands in 1917 and it was active until around 1931. De Stijl artists believed that art was about more than representing the world around us—it was a spiritual experience. De Stijl artists thought that the only way art could represent the spiritual was for it to mirror the harmony and order of math—so only squares, rectangles, and horizontal and vertical straight lines were used and only pure primary colors (red, yellow, and blue) and black and white were allowed. De Stijl art was abstract, which means it did not represent the world in a realistic way. In addition to painters there were De Stijl architects, poets, writers, and even furniture makers.

Divisionism: see **Pointillism**.

E

École des Beaux-Arts: The name given to a collection of famous art schools in France, the most well-known of which is in Paris. Many of France's most accomplished artists trained at the École des Beaux-Arts, including Edgar Degas, Claude Monet, and Georges Seurat.

Engraver: Someone who produces engravings. Engraving is a way of making a picture on paper with ink that can be copied many times. The image is cut with acid into a sheet of copper metal, called a plate. The plate is then covered in ink and the ink wiped off. The ink stays in the lines that have been cut into the plate. A damp sheet of paper is then placed on top of the plate and the plate and paper are put into a press. The ink in the cuts is transferred to the damp paper while it is pressed, producing a print.

F

Fresco: Painting directly onto the wet plaster of a wall. The artist has to work quickly and with as little error as possible so that he or she completes painting the section of the wall before it dries. Fresco paintings are very robust because they dry into the fabric of the wall.

G

Gautier, Theophile (1811–1872): An influential French journalist, playwright, critic, poet, painter, and novelist.

J

Japanese prints: Woodblock prints from Japan that were imported into Europe in large numbers during the nineteenth

century. These prints influenced European artists, who admired and copied their compositions and use of color and line.

Mannerist: Artwork that reflects Mannerism, a style of art that flourished in Europe, particularly in Italy, from about 1520 to 1580. Mannerism wasn't interested in depicting people, landscapes, plants, and animals in as realistic a way as possible but instead it showed these things in elongated forms, under dramatic lighting, and with lapses in perspective and scale. Mannerists used these techniques to represent the world in a way which they thought was more elegant and perfectly beautiful than the art which had gone before.

Medici, Ferdinando I de' (1549–1609): The Grand Duke of Tuscany and a great patron of the arts. The Medici family commissioned artists throughout the Renaissance, including Michelangelo and Leonardo da Vinci.

Michelangelo Buonarroti (1475–1564): An Italian painter, architect, sculptor, writer, and poet who, along with Leonardo da Vinci and Raphael Santi, is considered to be one of the greatest artists of the Italian Renaissance. Michelangelo's most famous work is the frescoed ceiling of the Sistine Chapel, the Pope's private chapel in the Vatican in Rome.

Neo-Plasticism: Another name for the De Stijl art movement.

Patron: Someone who employs artists such as painters, sculptors, composers, and musicians.

Pergola: A horizontal structure consisting of a trellis of poles or slats of wood supported on upright posts, used to support plants as they grow.

Picasso, Pablo (1881–1973): A Spanish painter and sculptor who is widely accepted as the greatest artist of the twentieth century. Picasso co-founded Cubism with Georges Braque and pioneered abstract painting.

Pointillism: A style of painting developed by the Post-Impressionist painter Georges Seurat. Pointillism was a painstaking style of painting that involved placing tiny dots of color next to each other so that from a distance the paint takes on the appearance of an entirely different color.

Raphael, Santi (1483–1520): An Italian painter and architect who is thought to be one of the three great masters of the Italian Renaissance, along with Michelangelo and Leonardo da Vinci. Raphael ran a large workshop and produced a great deal of work during his short lifetime (he died at the age of thirty-seven). His most famous works, the four Raphael Rooms, were done for Pope Julius II's palace in the Vatican, Rome.

Realist: A style of painting that originated in France in the nineteenth century. It aimed to depict exactly what the artist had seen. The Realists painted ordinary things, such as rural life and working people, rather than famous people, incidents from history, Classical mythology, or scenes from the Bible. The Realists painted in a rough style, applying the paint in a way that was meant to indicate that they had seen the thing they were depicting, rather than being restricted to working in a studio.

Suprematism: A short-lived Russian art movement founded in 1915 by Kazimir Malevich. Suprematism was based on geometric shapes, such as squares and circles, painted in starkly-contrasting colors, such as a black square floating on a white background, or a black circle floating on a white background. Suprematism became less popular in the 1920s but influenced later Russian art movements.

Vasari, Giorgio (1511–1574): An Italian painter and architect who wrote *Lives of the Most Excellent Painters, Sculptors, and Architects*, which was published in 1550. The *Lives of the Artists*, as it has come to be known, is an important source of information about Renaissance painting methods, techniques and artists and is one of the earliest books on Western art history.

Where to see the art in this book

Henri Matisse, *The Snail* Tate Gallery, London, UK

Georges Seurat, *The Circus* Musée d'Orsay, Paris, France

Lipunja, *Aboriginal Bark Painting* Musée du quai Branly, Paris, France

James Abbott McNeill Whistler, *Symphony in White No. III*
Barber Institute of Fine Arts, University of Birmingham, Birmingham, UK

Albrecht Dürer, *Portrait of Bernhard von Reesen* Gemaldegalerie Dresden, Germany

Jakob Van der Schley, *Buffel, Buffle* Buffalo Bill Historical Center, Cody, Wyoming, US

Theo van Doesburg, *Composition* Peggy Guggenheim Collection, Venice, Italy

Juan Gris, *Nature Morte; violon et verre* Musée National d'Art Moderne, Paris, France

Kazimir Malevich, *Suprematist Composition* Peggy Guggenheim Collection, Venice, Italy

Henri Rousseau, *Surprised!* National Gallery, London, UK

Jacopo Zucchi, *Pergola with Birds* Villa Medici, Rome, Italy

George Stubbs, *A Couple of Fox Hounds* Tate Gallery, London, UK

Index